A Witch's Primer
Grade: One

By: Lorin Manderly

authorHOUSE™

1663 LIBERTY DRIVE, SUITE 200
BLOOMINGTON, INDIANA 47403
(800) 839-8640
WWW.AUTHORHOUSE.COM

First published by AuthorHouse 09/29/05

ISBN: 1-4208-8320-8 (sc)

Printed in the United States of America
Bloomington, Indiana

This book is printed on acid-free paper.

Chapters:

Part One: Who We Are and What We Believe

Part Two: How We Live and the Worlds We Create

Dedicated To:

An imaginary friend.

Introduction

I wrote this book because I couldn't find one like it. I found a few books for adults who wanted to raise their children as Witches or other Pagans, but I couldn't find age-appropriate material for the children themselves that was realistic and honestly prepared them for studying the Craft. This is the first in a series of textbooks that will get progressively more advanced for each grade. My intent is to give the basics for each subject and prepare the students and their parents or teachers for seeking out further knowledge for the topics that interest them the most.

A long time dream of mine has been to open a private school for children being raised Pagan. It occurred to me recently that there were no text books for some of the subjects that such students would probably want to learn in such a place; and so – A Witch's Primer was born.

I recommend that parents read this book along with their children. I have included several safety warnings regarding the use of fire, knives, herbs, potions, etc.... but I want to include a note here as well. Under no circumstances do I recommend a child perform magick without a responsible adult's supervision. I also advise that any adults performing magick know exactly what they are doing beforehand.

That being said, I hope all readers enjoy! Learning can be fun when you are interested in the subject!
- Lorin Manderly

Chapter 1: The Goddess and The God

The World is made of a terrific Force. This Force has two sides: a female side and a male side. We call this female and male the **Goddess** and the **God**. They are *Deities*; which is another word for Gods.

We also call them Mother Goddess and Father God.

The Goddess and the God usually look just like us so that it is easy to talk to them, but they can look however we want them to. They can look different for everyone.

Can you draw what you want them to look like? What color is their skin? What color and shape are their eyes? What does their hair look like? Draw a face with eyes, nose and mouth and then color them in.

When you read about the Goddess and the God they might look young or old, or big or small. They are the same no matter what they look like. They are the same no matter where you live and no matter what you call them. They are a part of everything and everyone in the world. When you look at the sky, you are looking at the Father God. When you look at the land and the ocean, you are looking at the Mother Goddess. When you look at the sun, you are looking at the Father Sun God. When you look at the moon, you are looking at the Mother Moon Goddess.

Sometimes we talk about the Goddess and God as very young, and sometimes as very old. They are like people who start out as young children and grow older every year, but it only takes one year for them to grow from young to old. Then they start all over again.

We call the different ages of the Goddess: **The Maiden**, **The Bright and Dark Mother**, and **The Crone**.

We call the different ages of the God: **The Green Man**, **The Horned God**, and **The Oak and Holly King.**

The <u>Maiden</u> is very young. She is strong and beautiful. She is full of love. Her colors are white, pink and yellow; just like spring time. Imagine flowers in her hair and a twinkle in her eye. She is dancing barefoot and singing out loud. She loves to laugh.

We see the Maiden in the growing moon and in the new plants and flowers. She is friends with lots of animals. She is sometimes a warrior princess, and she is very brave.

Some words to describe the Maiden are: warrior, young, strong, spring-time, and waxing moon (or growing moon).

The <u>Mother</u> is both a <u>Bright Mother</u> and a <u>Dark Mother</u>. The Bright Mother has just left her young self and become an adult. She has just become the full moon. The Dark Mother has been an adult for a long time and will keep getting older. She has been the full moon and is starting to grow smaller again.

The Mother's colors are red and green. She is summer and fall. She is a parent to all children. She can heal when someone is sick or hurt. She can help plants to grow. She protects all of her children. She is loving and beautiful.

Some words to describe the Bright and Dark Mother are: grown-up, full-moon, parent, healer, protector, summer, and fall.

The <u>Crone</u> is the Goddess as an old woman. She is gentle and kind. She is very wise. She is also beautiful. Her colors are purple, black and grey. She is like the winter time. Imagine that she is like a grandmother who will welcome you into her home and tell you stories and secrets while showing you how to make cookies and homemade strawberry jam. She is like the moon that is getting smaller and smaller until it is completely gone and the night is dark. Soon the new moon can be born again.

Some words to describe the Crone are: Grandmother, waning moon, wise, story-teller, and winter-time.

The <u>Green Man</u> is young. He is strong and handsome. He is playful and joyous. He wears green leaves on his clothes and in his hair. He is like Robin Hood of the forest. He is strong. He is spring time. He likes music and poetry and dancing. He has a lively imagination! The trees and plants around the Green Man are young and bright and healthy. He loves to play!

Some words to describe the Green Man are: playful, green-leaves, Robin Hood, and spring-time.

The <u>Horned God</u> is the partner of the Mother Goddess. He is the father of everything. He is wise and handsome. He wears horns on his head and is related to the animals of the forest. He is also a hunter and in charge of the Wild Hunt.

He is summer time. He is wild and free and strong and healthy. He loves to be outside! Nature is the most wonderful thing to him. He likes to take care of those around him and he is a wonderful provider.

Some words to describe the Horned God are: summer-time, hunter, father, nature, and provider.

The <u>King</u> is both the <u>Oak King</u> and the <u>Holly King</u>. The Oak King is older than the Horned God. He is still strong, but he has grown older and is like the season of autumn. He is passionate about life and brings joy to those around him. He is surrounded by the colors of fall: reds, oranges, yellows. The Holly King is the Grandfather. He is happy to finally rest after a long life. He is a very wise and jolly man. He is like Santa Claus and is the winter season.

Some words to describe the Oak and Holly King are: autumn and winter-time, Santa Claus, grandfather, wise, and jolly.

What have we learned? The whole world, and the whole universe, came from one wonderful Force. This Force is both female and male; and we call the female Force, Goddess, and the male Force, God. They are Deities.

The Goddess and the God can look like anything we imagine. They can be any color or race or nationality. They can have long hair or short hair. They can be tall or short.

The Goddess is the moon and the earth and the water. The God is the sun and the sky.

The Goddess goes through three stages in her life. She starts as a Maiden and then becomes a Mother. She is first the Bright Mother and then the Dark Mother. Then she grows even older and becomes the Crone, before she starts life over again as the Maiden.

The God begins as the Green Man. As he becomes a grown-up, he becomes the Horned God. Finally he becomes the King: the Oak King when he is just reaching older age, and the Holly King when he is an old man and ready to start life over again as the Green Man.

Questions

1. What do we call the two sides of the Force?

2. What do they look like?

3. Which side represents the sun and the sky?

4. Which side represents the moon and the land and the ocean?

5. Who is the young Goddess?

6. Who is the grown-up Goddess?

7. Who is the oldest Goddess?

8. Who is the young God?

9. Who is the grown-up God?

10. Who is the oldest God?

Chapter 2: Many Goddesses, Many Gods

Witches often talk about many Goddesses and many Gods. First they talk about the Mother Goddess and the Father God that we learned about already, and then suddenly we hear them mention other Deities. We might hear someone talk about a Goddess named Diana or about a God who protects farmers. What's that about? Where did these extra Deities come from? They came from the Mother Goddess and Father God. They are the same. Have you ever seen a picture of a diamond that gives off a lot of sparkles?

That is what happens with the Goddess and the God, and all of the sparkles are other Deities.

Draw a picture below that is you. Then draw lines away from you like you are a diamond that is sparkling. Write a word on each of the lines. Make it a word that describes something you are good at or that you like to do. Like: Math, Swimming, or reading.

All of the things that you wrote about yourself are a part of you. Just like the extra Goddesses are parts of the Mother Goddess. If you wrote swimming down, that part of you is like **Poseidon** the sea God, who is a part of the Father God.

These parts of the Mother and Father Deities become whole Beings because we think of them that way. None of the Deities are better than the others, but they all have a talent or personality that makes them special. Just like us. When we need to borrow that special talent or feel that kind of personality, we can pray to whatever Deity fits our need. If you are a swimmer, you can pray to Poseidon to give you strength while you are in the water!

When we pray, we are *invoking,* or calling a Goddess or God. We are asking them to come to us. There are many reasons to talk to the Gods and Goddesses.

- Sometimes we need to know more than we do about our problems, and the Deities are much older and wiser than us.
- We might need the strength of someone special. Like someone who is really good with animals.

- Or maybe we just need someone to talk to, and we feel really close to one particular Goddess or God.

There are hundreds of them to choose from, and each one has its own personality. Each one has its own likes and dislikes. Some of them even have husbands and wives or brothers and sisters! Just like us!

It's important for all of us to learn more about both the Gods and the Goddesses. They help us to learn more about ourselves and how strong we are.

For girls, the Goddesses show us how beautiful and intelligent we can be, and that we can all be warriors! The Gods show girls how important it is to be strong and how to take charge when we have to!

For boys, the Gods show us how strong and smart we can be, and that we can all be wise men! The Goddesses show boys how important it is to be caring and how to help others when they need it!

Every culture throughout time has given names to their Deities. We put all of those from one place into a group, and we don't mix them up with other groups. You should work with them separately. Let's look at a few of those groups and at some of the Deities in them.

First let's talk about a few of the <u>Greek Deities</u>. We'll start with **Zeus**. **Zeus** is the king of the Greek Gods. He is the God of the sky and the clouds and the rain. He is older and has a beard. He carries a thunderbolt. He is very wise.

Hera is the wife of Zeus and the Queen of the Greek Gods. She is the Goddess of women. She is mature and beautiful. She wears a crown and carries a scepter.

Hecate is the Greek Goddess of the moon and of magick. She carries a torch and stands watching over wherever roads meet.

Apollo is the Greek God of hunting and healing. He is young and handsome. He carries a bow and arrows and rides a golden chariot.

Fortuna and **Janus** are two of the <u>Roman Gods</u>. **Cernunnos** and **Cerridwen** are <u>Celtic Gods</u>.

Fortuna is the Roman Goddess of fortune and fate. She carries a globe.

Janus is the Roman God of beginning and of doorways. He has two faces; one that can look into the past and one that looks into the future.

Cernunnos is the Horned God and the Universal Father. He has the horns of a stag on his head.

Cerridwen is another Goddess of the moon; and also of harvest and inspiration. She is the Crone and she stirs a cauldron of knowledge.

Isis and **Osiris** are <u>Egyptian Gods</u>. **Aradia** is an <u>Italian Goddess</u>, and **Freyja** is a <u>Norse Goddess</u>.

Isis is also a Mother Goddess of the moon and magick.

Osiris is her brother and he looks like a mummy with a human head. He is a God of vegetation.

Aradia is the Queen of the Witches in Italian tradition. She is very powerful and will protect you if you ask her to.

Freyja is the Norse Goddess of love and marriage. She is one of many love Goddesses. She rides a chariot drawn by cats.

What have we learned? There are many Gods and Goddesses, and they are all a part of the Father God and Mother Goddess, like sparkles of a diamond. These other Deities have their own personalities that make them special. They have likes and dislikes and talents just like us.

When we need to borrow strength or talent from a Deity, we can pray to them. Invoking a Deity is when you ask them to come to you. There are a lot of reasons to invoke the Gods and Goddesses.

There are hundreds of Deities and we should learn about them so that we can learn more about ourselves. The Gods and Goddesses are important for both boys and girls.

Every culture gives the Deities different names and we keep them in groups. Zeus, Hera, Hecate and Apollo are Greek Gods. Fortuna and Janus are Roman Gods. Cernunnos and Cerridwen are Celtic Gods. Isis and Osiris are Egyptian Gods. Aradia is the Queen of the Witches in Italy. Freyja is one of many love Goddesses. All of these are just a few examples of the many Deities in the world.

Questions

1. The many Gods and Goddesses are all part of the Father God and Mother Goddess, like the sparkles of a

    _____.

2. When you invoke a Deity, what are you asking them to do?

3. Do all of the Gods and Goddesses have their own personalities?

4. How many Deities are there? One, Three, or Hundreds? (Circle your answer.)

5. Goddesses show girls that they can all be _____.

6. Goddesses show boys how to be caring. True or False?

7. Gods show boys that they can all be

    _____.

8. Gods show girls how to be strong. True or False?

9. Every culture gives different _____ to their Deities.

10. Can you name one of the Deities we learned about in this chapter?

Chapter 3: The Spirit World

Everybody has an invisible friend! Did you know that? We call them **Spirit Guides**. Spirit Guides are sort of like Guardian Angels, but they stay here with us all of the time. They are our friends and teachers. We can have more than one Spirit Guide. In fact, we can have a lot!

Our Spirit Guides are a part of us and a part of where we came from. They have lived before, just like we are living now, and one day we will all meet again. For now they are invisible friends that guide us. They each have different talents and use those to help us with our talents. Sometimes they look like people, sometimes they look like animals. They are always good.

Spirit Guides are sent to watch out for us. They are also here to teach us about our life lessons. They are sent to be our friends and to help us behave. Do you know that little voice inside of you that tells you what is good and what is bad? That is your Spirit Guide.

Spirit Guides can keep us out of danger too. When your little voice is telling you to "watch out!" your Spirit Guide is trying to protect you. You should always pay attention to what your Spirit Guides are trying to tell you. You don't always have to follow that advice, because you will have to make your own decisions and take responsibility for them, but they are here to give advice when you need it. Sometimes things go better when we take the advice of others!

Our Spirit Guides can also help us find our life's job, and then help us to do it! They can even help us to understand the meaning of life if we ask them.

You can talk to them whenever you want to, though you might sometimes forget they are there. You can also see them in your dreams. They can come to you when you dream and give you messages or answers to questions that you ask.

What have we learned? Everyone has Spirit Guides. Our guides are like Guardian Angels and are always good. They are with us all of the time, even though we can't see them.

Spirit Guides do many things.

- They guide us.
- They teach us.
- They protect us.
- They share their talents with us.
- They help us find our life job.
- They help us with life lessons.
- They show us the meaning of life.

Spirit Guides can look like people or animals. We can see them when we dream. We can talk to them anytime we want, and in our dreams we can hear them talk to us.

We can hear them talk to us another way too: the little voice inside of us that tells us what is right and wrong is our Spirit Guide. Our Spirit Guides used to be alive, and one day we will all be together again.

Questions

1. Who has Spirit Guides?

2. When can we see our Spirit Guides?

3. What can our Spirit Guides help us find?

4. What can our Spirit Guides look like?

5. How do we hear our Spirit Guides while we're awake?

Chapter 4: Magickal People

There are a lot of different people who practice magick. All over the world and all through history, there have been families and groups who learn and do magick together and then teach it to others. If you are reading this book then you probably belong to one or more of these groups. We'll read about a few of these groups here.

First, let's talk about **Witches**. A Witch is someone who uses magick in their daily life and who follows the "Old Religion". A Witch connects with the energy in the Universe and uses it to make their magick work. A Witch believes in both a God and a Goddess.

The word *Witch* means "wise one". Witches spend their whole lives learning everything that they can and becoming very wise. They learn about nature and herbs and spirits, and many other things. Witches use nature to talk with the God and Goddess. They know that every tree and plant and piece of the Earth has the Mother Goddess and Father God inside of it.

Witches use herbs in their magick a lot. Herbs can be used to make a magickal drink. They can be burned to make a magickal smell. Herbs can also be turned into oils that magickally heal. Witches believe in spirits, and that they can work with them on their magick spells. Some Witches tell the future, and some celebrate magickal holidays and festivals.

Witches believe that if they are good, good things will happen to them, and if they are bad, bad things will come back to them. Another important thing to know: There have always been people who say that there is no such thing as Witches, but they never convince anyone. Since the beginning of time, people have always believed in Witches!

Another type of magickal person is the **Shaman**. A lot of people believe that Shamans were the first magickal people. Shamans are like Witches. They also talk to spirits and work with nature. Shamans work their magick with dancing and chanting and drumming.

People who practice **Voodoo** are usually from Africa or the Caribbean. Like Witches, they know that women and men are both important in magick. Healing is an important part of their magick.

One of the ways they use magick is in making poppets, or Voodoo dolls. These are little dolls made to look like a person they want to do magick for. If they want to heal a sick friend, they might make a poppet to look like their friend and then perform magick with the doll.

Druids are a secret group of priests. We don't know very much about them, but we do know that they lived a very long time ago. Some people have started practicing Druidry again today.

They were healers and they could tell the future. They were also poets who memorized all of their poetry instead of writing it down. They respected the Earth and worked with nature.

Gypsies are travelers who keep mostly to themselves within their own group or clan. They used to live in wagons on wheels that were beautifully decorated. These were called *vardos*.

All of the Gypsies in a clan would travel in their vardos together and set up camp somewhere. Wherever they set up camp they would sell their magick to the people in the nearby towns.

They told fortunes by reading palms and cards. They would also do magick spells. They lived out in nature and believed in the magick of the wild. Magick was part of their entire life.

After they had stayed for a while in one place, all of the Gypsies in the clan would pack up their vardos and move on to the next place and perform their magick there.

What have we learned? There have always been magickal people in the world. A lot of these people practice their magick with their families or in groups. They also teach their magick to the other people in their family. There are many different groups that live magickal lives.

Witches have always been around. They use their magick in their normal lives. <u>Witch</u> means "wise one", and Witches spend their whole lives learning. Witches use nature and herbs and spirits to work their magick. Some Witches tell the future and some celebrate magickal holidays. They believe that being good brings them good luck, and being bad brings them bad luck.

Shamans might have been the first magick people. They use chanting, drumming and dancing in their magick.

People who practice Voodoo sometimes make poppets, or little dolls, to use during their magick.

Druids are a secret group. They are healers and poets.

Gypsies travel with their families and friends from place to place. They used to travel in vardos. They sell their magick spells and fortune-telling to people when they travel.

Questions

1. How long have there been magickal people?

2. Some magickal people work with groups or with their families. True or False.

3. What does the word "Witch" mean?

4. Can you name at least one thing that Witches do with herbs?

5. What do Witches think will happen if they do good things?

6. Shamans like to use chanting and dancing and _____ in their magickal practices.

7. The dolls used in Voodoo are called

   _____ .

8. Druids were also poets, but they didn't write their poems down. What did they do instead?

9. What are the wagons that Gypsies travel in called?

10. Name one of the ways that Gypsies tell the future.

Chapter 5: History of Magick

Witches have been around for a very long time. They have worshipped the God and the Goddess and nature as part of their religion – **the Old Religion** – for longer than any other religion has been around. The magick that Witches practiced at the beginning of time was mostly about working with the Deities to help find food and shelter.

We know that the Old Religion has been around for this long because there are pictures on the walls of caves; drawn by people who lived in them at the beginning of the human race. The drawings are of people dressed up like animals with horns who are dancing. This is similar to when witches today act like the Horned God during their ceremonies.

There have also been clay statues found of different Deities that were made *thousands* of years ago!

When the Christian religion started, its leaders tore down the places where the magickal people practiced their Old Religion. They built their own churches on the same spots so that they could trick people who believed in the old ways into coming there still and becoming a Christian.

The people weren't fooled though. They pretended to be Christian, but then still practiced their own ways – in secret.

The new church officials told people that the Horned God was the devil and very bad. There had never been a devil in the Old Religion. The Horned God was a good God. It wasn't until the Christian leaders came along that our God became the "bad guy". They made the whole thing up!

Magickal people knew that this wasn't true, but the church leaders made it against the law to pray to the Horned God and the Goddess. They said that anyone who believed in many Deities or who practiced Magick was evil and must be punished. They made everyone very afraid.

People began to believe that Witches were bad. This was not true though. Witchcraft was always about love of nature and the joy of living.

People were so afraid though, that they started calling each other Witches just to get them into trouble. Most of these people were not really Witches at all. The real Witches started keeping it a secret that they practiced magick. The only reason that magick stayed alive was because the grown-ups taught it to their children and wrote it all down in secret, private books called their **Book of Shadows.**

Finally, not too long ago, the laws were changed. Being a Witch was legal again!

Ever since it became okay again to be magick, more and more people have started practicing Witchcraft out in the open. More people are choosing to learn about Witchcraft too.

We all love being open and honest about who we are and what we believe!

There is an important lesson that we have to know about the troubles that Witches and the people who practice the Old Religion went through. It's not okay to tell people what they can and cannot believe in. Everyone is allowed to make that choice for themselves. Even you! Witches do not hate Christians. We don't like it when someone tells us that our way is wrong or that we will get into trouble for our beliefs; but when someone says this to us, we just walk away. We know that they just have different beliefs than us, and that's okay!

What have we learned? Witches have practiced their religion - the old religion - for longer than any other religion has been around. There have been cave drawings and clay statues found that prove that thousands of years ago people practiced magick and believed in the God and the Goddess.

When the Christian religion started, the leaders wanted to get rid of the old religion and stop Witches from practicing magick. They tore down all of the places where we worshipped and they rebuilt their own churches on the same spots. Christian leaders thought that they could make everyone become a Christian. They started making laws that said practicing magick was very bad and that Witches had to be punished. They told everyone that the Horned God was the devil.

Soon everyone was so afraid by what the officials were telling them that they started accusing other people of being Witches, just to get them into trouble. A lot of people got into trouble because of this, and most of them were not really Witches. The real Witches kept their beliefs a secret from everyone but their families. Magick was kept alive by teaching it in secret to the children and by writing it down in the Book of Shadows.

Witches don't believe that anyone has the right to tell us what to think or believe. We don't stay mad at Christians for the mistakes made so long ago. We accept that everyone has the right to make their own decision about what to believe in.

Questions

1. The religion of Witches is sometimes called the _____.

2. Pictures of people dressed like animals have been found in _____.

3. The cave drawings are like the Witches who act like whom?

4. Which religion tried to wipe out Witchcraft and the Old Religion when they first started?

5. What did the new church officials say about the Horned God?

6. Why did people start calling each other Witches?

7. Most of the people who got into trouble for being a Witch were not really Witches at all. True or False?

8. Magick stayed alive because the grown-ups taught it to whom?

9. The books where Witches wrote down their secrets and beliefs were called the _____.

10. Witches believe that everyone should be allowed to choose their own religion and beliefs. True or False?

Chapter 6: Myths and Legends

People always pass down stories to their family and friends about their adventures. Pretty soon so many people have heard and retold these stories that everyone knows about them. Sometimes a story has been around for so long and been told in so many ways that we don't know if it's true or not. These stories are called **myths** and **legends**.

Every culture throughout the ages has had their own collection of myths and legends that have been told and retold over and over again. Each culture chooses to believe certain stories, and those become the history and religion of that culture. They could be right to believe: there is no proof that these stories are true or false. You can believe, or not believe, in which ever myths and legends feel important to you.

Some of the most famous myths and legends are the *Arthurian* tales. These are the stories about **King Arthur** of Camelot and all of the knights, ladies and magicians who lived there with him. In this chapter we are going to learn about some of the Arthurian myths and legends.

First, there was a place called **Avalon**.
<u>Avalon</u> means *"Apple Isle"*, and it is the name
of a magickal, mysterious island. Avalon is
hidden in the water and covered with mist,
so no one can find it unless they belong
there.

Living on the island of Avalon are the
Priestesses who study the magick of the
Goddess. They also study healing and
medicine and how to control the weather.
The Chief Priestess of Avalon is also called
the **Lady of the Lake**, and she protects the
magickal sword **Excalibur**. There have been
many Ladies of the Lake, including **Nimue**
and **Morgan le Fay**.

Excalibur is one of many magickal swords
in myths and legends. The first time it was
heard of is when the wizard named **Merlin**
told the people that whoever could take
Excalibur for themselves would be the King.
Up until that time the sword would stay stuck
inside a stone and would be guarded by the
Lady of the Lake.

Merlin was a very wise and powerful
wizard. He worked closely with the Ladies of
the Lake and fell in love with the Lady named
Nimue. Merlin knew that one day the sword
Excalibur would be claimed by the future
King, Arthur. When Arthur was born Merlin
took him to a secret foster family where no
one would know he was the future King and
where he could live and be safe until he was
grown.

Arthur lived with his foster father and brother, Sir Ector and Sir Kay, until he was old enough to be King. Arthur's sister, **Morgan le Fay**, grew up on Avalon learning magick and being trained in the ways of the Goddess so that one day she could be a Lady of the Lake. Merlin told their parents that they had to grow up in these different places so that they could one day be a great King and a great Priestess who would follow the ways of the Goddess even though the Christian religion was growing stronger.

One day Arthur was finally old enough to be King. He built his Kingdom and called it **Camelot**; and he married a beautiful lady named **Guinevere**. Camelot became the most wonderful Kingdom you could ever imagine.

Arthur ruled Camelot with honor and fairness, and he wanted all of the knights in his Kingdom to be good, heroic men. He built a huge round table for them to sit at and he called them the **Knights of the Round Table.**

King Arthur's knights were the best knights in all the world and he made their meeting table round to show that they were all equally important. There was no "head of the table".

Some of the most famous knights were: **Sir Lancelot**, **Sir Gawain**, **Sir Percival**, and **Sir Galahad**.

Sir Lancelot was the greatest fighter, and when he came to Camelot he became the best knight of all. He married the Lady Elaine and had a son named **Galahad**.

Sir Gawain was the knight who fought the Green Knight. He became a champion of women, and always fought to keep women safe.

Sir Percival went to Camelot as a very young man after he heard about the Knights of the Round Table. He had to work at the castle and earn the right to be a knight. He became one of the greatest knights and was one of the **"Three Elect"** who found the **Holy Grail**.

Sir Galahad was the son of the best knight Sir Lancelot, and after his father knighted him, Galahad became the *most perfect* knight. Sir Galahad was destined to achieve the **Holy Grail**, and he was one of the **"Three Elect"**.

The **Holy Grail** is a symbol of the God and Goddess. It is a magickal goblet that can heal the sick and feed the hungry. It is a cauldron that gives people knowledge of everything there is to know in the world.

All of the Knights of the Round Table dreamed of going on the quest to find the Grail that had been lost for such a long time. They all traveled in different directions to find it.

The Grail is guarded by the **Fisher King** – a title that is given to different men throughout the ages. Sir Percival and Sir Galahad were related to past Fisher Kings.

The **"Three Elect"** are the three knights who finally found the Grail: **Sir Galahad**, **Sir Percival**, and **Sir Bors**. They found the Grail because they were the most *pure of heart*.

Sir Galahad was the only person able to drink from the Grail because he was completely good in thought and deed. After he drank from it he was filled with all knowledge and he disappeared with the Grail out of the human world and into the world of the Goddess and God.

Sir Percival became the new Fisher King.

When King Arthur was dying and Camelot was ending, a knight named Sir Bedivere took Arthur and his sword Excalibur to the lake where Avalon is hidden. Out of the mist came a boat with three women on it. One of the women was Arthur's sister, Morgan le Fay. The women took Arthur back to Avalon with them so that he could recover from his wounds and rest there until the world was ready for him to come back.

What have we learned? Myths and legends are stories that cannot be proven true or false. Each culture decides over the years which stories they will believe in, and that is how the history and religion of a culture is born. If a story feels important to you, then you can believe in it.

The Arthurian stories are very famous myths and legends. These stories are about King Arthur and the Knights of the Round Table.

Arthur and his sister Morgan le Fay were both raised by people who helped them grow up to be a great King and one of the Ladies of the Lake. The Lady of the Lake protects the sword Excalibur and is the Chief Priestess on the island of Avalon; a magickal island that is hidden in the mist. Excalibur is the sword that will prove that Arthur is meant to be King.

Merlin was the famous wizard who took Arthur and Morgan to their foster homes.

When Arthur grew up he married Guinevere and built a Kingdom he called Camelot. He made sure his knights were all the best and bravest. Sir Lancelot was the best knight. Sir Gawain fought for women. Sir Percival worked at the castle to earn the title of knight. Sir Galahad was Lancelot's son and the most perfect knight of all.

The Holy Grail is a symbol of the God and Goddess. It is magickal and can only be found by the pure of heart. The Grail is guarded by the man who is the Fisher King. The "Three Elect" are the three knights who found the Grail.

Sir Galahad was the only one so pure that he could drink from the Grail, and afterward he went to join the Goddess and God.

When King Arthur was dying he went to Avalon to rest and recover with his sister, until the world needed them again.

Questions

1. What are Myths and Legends?

2. Who are the Arthurian legends about?

3. Who is Arthur's sister?

4. Where did Morgan le Fay grow up?

5. What is the name of King Arthur's sword?

6. Who was the famous wizard that took Arthur and his sister to live in their foster homes?

7. What is the name of King Arthur's Kingdom?

8. Where did Arthur's knights sit?

9. Who was the best knight?

10. Who was the most perfect knight?

11. Who guards the Holy Grail?

12. What are the three knights who found the Grail called?

13. Which of the "Three Elect" became a Fisher King?

Chapter 7: The Circle of Life

Most Witches believe that we were already alive before we were born. We believe in **reincarnation.** That means that we live over and over again, learning new lessons and experiencing new adventures; and that after we die we are reborn as a new person. In each of our lifetimes we have to complete a **circle of life**.

The place that our Spirit can be found before we are born is called the **Summerland.** It is a beautiful, peaceful place with mountains and trees and rivers, and perfect weather.

While we live there we have the chance to rest our Spirit and to think about the life we just finished. Then we decide what kind of life we are going to live next, and what lessons we want to learn in that life. We will keep coming back until every lesson has been learned and we are ready to go back to the Goddess and God. That is what living is all about. The circle of life that we follow is: **birth**, **growth**, **death**, and **rebirth**.

We are **born** into a life and a family that we chose when we were in the Summerland. In each of our lives we stay with a lot of the same people. Someone who was your friend last time might be your mom or dad now!

Once we are born, the people in our lives celebrate our arrival. Sometimes there are parties, sometimes there are spiritual ceremonies. These celebrations are to welcome the new child into the community and to ask the God and Goddess to watch over them. This is the wonderful beginning of a new life!

Every day we are **growing**. Yes, when we are children we grow bigger until we are grown up; but we are growing on the inside too. We grow smarter and we learn how to be people in the world. During our lives we have different important times of growing. We stop doing baby things and start doing big-kid things. We start going to school. We finish school and get a job. We move out into the world and have many adventures. Some of us get married and bring other children into the world. While we are having these experiences in growing we are becoming wiser and learning the lessons we came here to do. The growing part of the circle of life is the longest and most important part. This is when we do everything that we were brought to life to do. Growing up and growing closer to the Goddess and God is the job they assigned you before you left the Summerland.

Some people think that **death** is bad or scary. This is not true. It doesn't happen until we've done our job of growing and our Spirits are ready to go back to the Summerland; and only the Goddess and God can decide when that is.

When we get to the Summerland it is beautiful and peaceful. It is filled with flowers and gardens and magick, like Avalon of the Arthurian legends. We are greeted into the Summerland by the family and friends who go before us, and we all have a great big party together. Then we think back over our life and everything we did. After we have done all of this and we've rested our spirits, we decide when it's time to move on. When it is time, we do one of two things: if we have more lessons to learn, a part of us is born again into a new life. If we have finished learning and growing, we join the God and Goddess.

Rebirth makes us a little bit different than the person we were in the last life. The Spirit of who we were before stays in the Summerland, and a new piece of us moves on. Do you remember the diamond with all of the sparkles that we talked about when we were learning about many Gods and Goddesses? Now imagine that the center, big diamond is where you came from. This is the _real_ you. All of the sparkles are your different lives. In your next life you will be another sparkle. You will be different, but you will still be the same diamond! Now it is time to start the whole circle of life over again.

What have we learned? Every one of us goes through the **Circle of Life**. That means that we are born, we grow, we die, and then we are reborn again. To be reborn again is called **reincarnation**. When we are waiting to be reborn we live in the **Summerland**. The Summerland is a beautiful and peaceful place where we rest our Spirits. While we are there we think about our past life and then choose our next one.

When we are born we are celebrated by our family and friends. These celebrations welcome us into the world.

When we are growing we are doing the job that we were born to do. We have different adventures and experiences that bring us closer to the Goddess and God. Each of us spends our growing time learning many lessons.

When it is time to die it is because we have finished learning our lessons and the God and Goddess have decided we are ready to go back to the Summerland. This is not a bad thing; it is a part of our circle of life. When we get to the beautiful Summerland we are greeted by our loved ones who have gone before us.

Once we have rested our souls, we look back over the life we have just lived and the things that we did. If there are more lessons for us to learn, then we go on to live a brand new life. If we have learned everything we need to, then we go on to join the Goddess and God.

Even though we are a different person when we are reborn we are still a part of who we've always been. Every one of our lifetimes is like a sparkle in the diamond of who we are!

<u>Questions</u>

1. What are the four parts of the Circle of Life?

2. What does reincarnation mean?

3. When we're waiting to be born, where do we live?

4. Why do people celebrate when we are born?

5. When we are growing, who are we getting closer to?

6. Who are we greeted by when we return to the Summerland?

7. If there are more lessons for us to learn after we've rested our souls, what do we do?

8. If we've learned everything we need to, who do we go back to?

Chapter 8: The Holidays

Witches believe in celebration! We have eight big holidays during each year. We also celebrate the good things that happen to us – like birthdays and weddings and babies and even the full moon – in a big way! Our holidays are called the **Sabbats** and the **Esbats**.

Esbats are the days that Witches meet to celebrate, that aren't official holidays. It is usually when the moon is full. There are thirteen full moons in one year. Witches believe that our connection to the Goddess and God is strongest on the nights of the full moon. The full moon is a symbol of the Goddess as the mother of the earth. Many Witches hold celebrations every time the moon is full.

Sabbats are the eight major holidays. The holidays celebrate the birth, growth, death, and rebirth of the earth through the Mother Goddess. We can see this circle of life of the earth in the changing seasons. We hold festivals on each of the Sabbats to celebrate each stage of the earth's life and each new season. These stages of life are different points on the **Wheel of Life**. One full turn of the wheel equals one year.

When we celebrate our festivals we are honoring the God and Goddess as the father and mother of the earth. The festivals help us to grow closer to nature and give us a chance to thank the Goddess and God for everything they give us all year long.

We put aside our work and we have great parties. Sometimes we wear special costumes and certain colors. We decorate to show the season with flowers and leaves; and we say prayers that are written for the holiday we are celebrating. We feast on delicious food and drink and play games or dance to show how much we love life.

Some of our holidays are just like the ones you've been celebrating all of your life, and some of them will be very new. The most important thing about all of them is to celebrate!

Samhain

How to say it: (Sow [like cow] - Win)

When it is: October 31ˢᵗ = Samhain Eve
                November 1ˢᵗ = Samhain

What it is: I'll bet you've been celebrating this holiday your whole life! It's also known as *Halloween* or *All Hallow's Eve.* This is one of the most important holidays for Witches! This is our *New Year's.* On Samhain Eve our old year ends, and on Samhain our new year begins. It's sometimes called "summer's end". The earth is now starting to die, so that the land can rest and prepare to be reborn again when planting season comes. For now, farming is over.

How we celebrate:
- We feast! Some of the foods we eat on Samhain are: pumpkin, squash, apples, corn on the cob, warm breads, pork, soup and sweets!
- We decorate with jack-o-lanterns and ghosts and the colors of fall. The colors of fall are orange, red, yellow, and black.
- We honor our loved ones who are already in the Spirit world. On this night it is easier to talk with the spirits than at any other time. We ask them to bless our year ahead and to help us tell fortunes about what will happen to us. We thank them for their love and then we celebrate with them on this night of magick!

Yule

<u>How to say it</u>: (Yool)
<u>When it is</u>:   December 20th, 21st, or 22nd

<u>What it is</u>: This holiday is what most people call Christmas. Yule is very close to the same thing; it just happens a few days earlier and it's about the earth and the God and Goddess. It's sometimes called the *Winter Solstice*. Yule is the time when the year and the sun are ready to be reborn. Ever since Summer time came to an end, the days have been shorter and the nights have been longer. At Yule this will start to change. The **Wheel of the Year** is turning and slowly the days will grow longer and the nights will be shorter.

<u>How we celebrate</u>:
- We decorate our homes with magickal things that will encourage spring time to return. Holly, ivy and pine represent life. We hang them on our doors and in our homes for protection. We hang mistletoe to bring love to our lives and families. We put up pine and fir trees because they mean strength and life: they are the trees that stay green during the winter time and they will lead the other plants back to life.
- We also decorate with lights and candles to represent the sun and our need for the sun

to return. The colors we use at Yule are red, green, gold, white and silver.

- Some of the fun things we do at Yule are: caroling, exchanging presents, and burning the Yule log. The Yule log is a newly cut log that we gather on Yule Eve and bring to our home. We let it burn to give the sun power.
- We play music and visit with family. Everything is about peace, joy, and celebration; and of course, the feast! We eat cookies, cakes, turkey, ham, oranges, eggnog, and cider among many other wonderful dishes.

Imbolc

How to say it: (Em-Bolk)
When it is: February 2nd

What it is: A celebration that the year is beginning to grow up. Today we honor the Goddess for turning the wheel closer to spring time. This day is sometimes called the *Festival of Lights* or the *Festival of Brigid*. Brigid is a Goddess of poetry and spring time who watches over flocks of animals and new-born babies. She also blesses people who give to charity. This is a day when we can really begin to feel the sun again. The symbols of Imbolc are brides, sun-wheels, grain dolls, and candles.

How we celebrate:
- On the eve of Imbolc we light candles and put them in every window and let them burn until sunrise.
- On Imbolc day we weave a "Brigid's Cross" out of straw and hang it in our home until next Imbolc. These will make our minds and spirits strong.
- We go outside and search for signs of the spring time and we bless the seeds we will plant when the spring time comes.
- We also march in small, noisy parades so that the spring will be sure to wake up.

- The colors of Imbolc are white, yellow, and pink; and these are the colors of the candles we will light. Tonight we will light more candles and a big sacred bonfire that will call out to the sun. Sometimes we make sun-wheels out of grain to honor the sun as well.
- Of course, we don't forget to feast! On this holiday we eat a lot of dairy foods, as well as honey and poultry and a lot of spicy things. Some of us drink something called: *Lambswool.* – Don't worry, that's just a hot drink made of crabapples and spices!

Ostara

How to say it: (Oh-Star-Uh)
When it is: March 20th, 21st, or 22nd

What it is: Ostara is the *Spring Equinox*. On this day, both day-light and darkness are equal. This is the first day of spring – when the earth is finally waking up. The symbols of Ostara are the new moon, colored eggs, rabbits, and all new-born animals. This day is about the beginning of new life. Eggs represent life, and so do rabbits. Newborn animals remind us of new beginnings. You probably used to think of this day as Easter.

How we celebrate:
- This is when we throw open our windows and let the sunshine in.
- We might start our day by lighting a fire as the sun comes up. Then, as the day grows later, we will decorate our homes with the colors green, yellow and pink, and with fresh flowers and herbs.
- We will color eggs to eat, and later we will take the egg shells that we save and throw them into the new gardens. Their magick will bring life to the seeds we will plant.
- Today we will start our planting of vegetables or herbs, for all witches should add to the cycle by growing something;

even if it's just a potted plant in the window.

- Our feast will have eggs and waffles, fruits, honey- cakes, green vegetables, and hot-cross buns!

Beltane

How to say it: (Bell-Tane)
When it is: April 30th

What it is: The arrival of summer! This day
is sometimes called *May Day*, and when it
arrives it means that the earth is fully awake
and blossoming. This is the time of year
when the God and Goddess are **handfast**
in union. A **handfasting** is the way Witches
get married; and this time of year is all
about love, friendship, peace and prosperity.
Beltane is when we plant the rest of the food
and herbs that haven't been started yet. The
symbols of Beltane are flowers, bells, May
baskets, and May poles.

How we celebrate:
- On the day of Beltane there is a lot of
  music, dancing, feasting and drinking.
  Some of the foods we eat are: strawberries,
  cherries, salads, Beltane cakes, oatmeal
  cakes, custard, and ice cream.
- We decorate with crowns of flowers and
  with the colors red, white, blue, lavender,
  green and yellow.
- There are two important and fun
  traditions for the Beltane holiday: **Bringing
  in the May** and the **May Pole Dance**.
- For **Bringing in the May**, all of the
  children go out at midnight on April 30th

and gather baskets of flowers. When they have as many flowers as they can hold, they come back to their homes as a group. They stop at each of their houses to leave some of their flowers and to shout *"Bringing in the May!"* In return, the adults in each house give to them their best food and drink. Once the adults do this, the children bless their house.

- **Dancing around the May Pole** is done on May 1st. Large poles are put into the earth so that they are sticking straight up into the air. Colored ribbons are attached to the tops of the May Poles, and on top of the ribbons are wreaths of flowers. Everyone stands in a circle around the pole: boy, girl, boy, girl; and each holds onto one of the ribbons attached to the pole. While music plays, the boys and men dance clockwise around the pole and the girls and women dance counter-clockwise. Everyone takes turns at dancing under each other's ribbons until all of the ribbons are wound tightly around the pole and the wreath of flowers slides down to the ground.

Midsummer

How to say it: (Mid-Summer)
When it is: June 20th, 21st, or 22nd

What it is: The longest day of the year.
Midsummer is exactly that: the middle of
summer. The sunlight will last longer today
than any other day of the year; and tomorrow
the days will start to grow shorter again.
Sometimes this day is called the *Summer
Solstice*, and it is truly a day of celebrating
the sun. Everything around us is beautiful
and green. Our gardens have been growing,
and now we can start to pick the vegetables
and herbs. Midsummer's symbols are the
sun, fire, oak trees, and faeries.

How we celebrate:
- The colors we use at Midsummer are
  green, gold, blue and tan.
- The foods we feast on are the foods of
  summer: summer fruits, like watermelon;
  summer vegetables, like corn on the cob;
  summer greens in nice, leafy salads;
  barbeque; and fun, picnic foods.
- Midsummer is a perfect day for a picnic;
  and we can start by collecting some of
  the good fruits and vegetables from our
  gardens to take with us.
- One of the most important activities of
  Midsummer is the bonfire we will light as
  the sun starts to go down. A bonfire is our
  tribute to the sun.

Lammas

<u>How to say it</u>: (Lah-Muss)
<u>When it is</u>:   August 1st

<u>What it is</u>: The God is growing older and losing his strength. Though the days are still long and hot, we can tell that the nights are getting colder and a little longer. It is almost the season of fall. Now is the time of hope for a good harvest season. We celebrate the bounty of things we have grown, as well as the bounty – or successes – in our lives. This holiday is also called *The Feast of Bread*, because this is when we finally pick the grains from the field to make bread with. The grains and fruits are fully grown and ready to be harvested. The symbols of Lammas are baskets of bread, sheaves of grain, corn dollies, cauldrons, fire, and dried herbs.

<u>How we celebrate</u>:
- At Lammas we start our morning by gathering the grain. Later that day we will bake our bread. Don't forget to give the first loaf to the God and Goddess!
- A tradition at Lammas is to hold country faires and markets: to meet up with old friends, make new ones, and to sell and trade the things we've made and grown.
- We will also play games of sport with our friends.

- Our feast will be of wheat, oat and corn bread; as well as squash, corn, potatoes, plumbs, berries and acorns.

Mabon

How to say it: (May-Bon)
When it is: September 21st

What it is: Fall is finally here. Other names for Mabon are: *The Harvest*, the *Autumn Equinox*, and the *Feast of Avalon*. The earth is starting to get colder so we will finish harvesting everything we've grown, and store it for the Winter. Then we will rest and feast and give thanks to the earth. This day is sort of like the Witches' Thanksgiving. Day and night are equal again and now we will see the nights grow slowly longer than the days. The symbols of Mabon are harvest symbols: autumn leaves and flowers, acorns, grapes, and trees whose leaves have fallen.

How we celebrate:
- The colors of Mabon are red, gold, orange, yellow, purple and brown.
- More important than anything else at Mabon is the feast. We gather with our family and friends and eat until we are stuffed!
- Some of the foods are: cornbread, wheat bread, grains, berries, grapes, squash, carrots, potatoes, pomegranates, goose, and mutton.
- Aside from all of the wonderful foods we eat, we also get to know our family and

friends again during long walks in nature and by talking about what we're thankful for.

What have we learned? Witches have their own holidays, and we celebrate every one of them in a big way. We see life as a wheel that turns; and one complete turn equals one year. The holidays that Witches celebrate are about nature, the changing of the seasons, and the life of the God and Goddess. We call the eight holidays the Sabbats. Some Witches also celebrate the thirteen full moons in the year. These are called the Esbats. When we celebrate, we honor the God and Goddess and grow closer to nature. All of our holidays have two things in common: we always have a feast and we always do something to connect us to nature.

Samhain is like Halloween. It is on October 31st and November 1st. It is the Witches' New Year; and is the day of the year when it is easiest to communicate with our deceased loved ones.

Yule is like Christmas. It is on December 20th, 21st, or 22nd. It's the Winter Solstice, and it happens when the year and the sun are ready to be reborn. An important tradition at this time is burning the Yule log.

Imbolc is on February 2nd. It is the celebration of the year beginning to grow up. It is sometimes called the Festival of Brigid. We celebrate by searching for spring time.

Ostara is the Spring Equinox, and is on March 20th, 21st, or 22nd. Day light and darkness are equal this day. It is the first day of spring and we celebrate by honoring all new life. We plant some of our first herbs and vegetables today.

Beltane is on April 30th. It means that summer has arrived. This is when the God and Goddess are handfast, and when we plant the rest of our food and herbs and grains. Two important traditions at this time are Bringing in the May and the May Pole Dance.

Midsummer is June 20th, 21st, or 22nd. This is the longest day of the year, and after this the days will start to get shorter again. Tonight's feast will include a huge bonfire that represents the sun.

Lammas is August 1st. It is almost the fall. This is also called the Feast of Bread, and we celebrate by picking the first grains and making bread. We also hold country faires and markets to sell our homemade goods.

Mabon means that fall is finally here. It is September 21st, and it is the Autumn Equinox. This day is the Witches' Thanksgiving. We harvest everything we've planted and we give thanks to the earth.

Questions

1. What does one turn of the *Wheel of Life* equal?

2. Name one of the three things that the holidays are about.

3. What are the eight major holidays called?

4. What do we call the thirteen full moons?

5. What Witches' holiday is like Halloween?

6. Which holiday is also called the Winter Solstice?

7. Which festival is another name for Imbolc?

8. Which holiday is on the first day of spring?

9. What arrives with Beltane?

10. Which holiday sees a huge bonfire representing the sun?

11. When do we usually hold country faires and markets?

12. What do we call the Witches' Thanksgiving?

Chapter 9: A Witch and Their Household

Witches are people who learn how to do magick, and who use it in their daily lives. You might wonder if magick is real. The answer is yes! Magick is around us all of the time; and anyone can do it. Magick is when you use your mind and your own energy to make the energy outside of yourself do as you wish. Witches learn how to do this and spend the rest of their lives practicing and growing more powerful.

Witches believe that nature is sacred. We love nature in all of its forms and believe it must be protected. Some of us do this by cleaning up litter off of the ground. Some of us live near the natural outdoors and work to keep the trees and flowers alive and healthy. Some Witches grow natural fruits and vegetables for others to eat. No matter what we do, Witches all believe that keeping the natural earth safe and healthy is one of our most important daily jobs.

Some people today keep it a secret that they are a Witch. This could be because their family and friends don't yet know they are Witches. It could also be because they are afraid of what people would think of them. Whether you decide to tell people you are a Witch or whether you keep it a secret, is your choice. However, whatever you decide will affect the way you live your daily life.

Some of us like to fill our homes with objects that are magickal or that represent the Deities we work with. There are certain rituals and festivals that are celebrated out in the open. These things would be difficult to do if we were afraid of being found out as a Witch. We all would like to live our lives as Witches out in the open, without hiding the way we pray, the way we practice magick, or our love for the Goddess.

Even though Witches believe that everyone should be allowed to live as they please, we do follow a few rules. The most important one of these is called **The Rede**. That rule says: *"And it harms none, do as you will"*. This means that we are free to do whatever we want, as long as it doesn't hurt anyone in any way. We are not allowed to hurt anyone physically, emotionally, or any other way. We are also not allowed to hurt ourselves. The Witch's Rede is the first rule you should always remember.

Witches believe in being good and making the world a better place. Of course, no one is good all of the time, but what matters is that we try our hardest every day to do good and make the right decisions. That is how it works: each day we decide how we are going to behave and what we will do for the world and other people. Remember this: every single thing that we do, comes back to us *times three.*

The **Rule of Three** is the belief that when we do good, three times that amount of good will come back to us; and also that when we do bad, three times that amount of bad will come back to us. This is also an example of **Karma. Karma** is the word that describes how everything that happens to us is because of something we've done in the past.

There is a lot more to a Witch's daily life than following a few rules. Most of us like to create something sacred in our homes, or even an *entirely* sacred home. We might start with something as simple as the decorations on our walls and the books on our shelves. Most Witches also have an **Altar** some place in their homes. The household Altar is a special place that is kept separate from ordinary things. This is where we say our prayers and honor the God and Goddess; where we sit to feel calm and safe. Our Altars are decorated with objects that represent our Deities, our beliefs, and the season we are celebrating.

We can also make our homes sacred every day with the things we bring into them. For instance, a lot of the magick that Witches do is in the kitchen. Whether making oils and potions, baking the festival bread, or cooking the family dinner, Witches put their magickal energy into the job. A lot of us use home grown and organic foods. Witches like for their lives to be as close to nature as they can be, no matter where they live; and by growing our own fruits and vegetables or in buying organic foods that are grown naturally, we can do this.

What have we learned? A Witch's life and household is full of magick every day. Magick is made with our minds and energy, and the energy of the Universe. Witches spend their whole lives practicing their magick.

Witches believe that nature is sacred and they do many things to keep the natural earth safe and healthy.

There are still people who keep it a secret that they are Witches. There are some parts of being a Witch that are harder to do when you keep this secret; like rituals, festivals and practicing magick.

The rules that Witches live by are called **The Rede** and **The Rule of Three**. The Rede says *"And it harms none, do as you will"*; which means that a person can do whatever they wish, as long as they do not harm anyone. The Rule of Three says that everything we do will come back to us times three. **Karma** is what happens to us because of the things we do, whether good or bad.

Some of the things you might find in a Witch's home are: an Altar to pray and worship at, magickal books and decorations, and natural, organic foods.

Questions

1. What two parts of ourselves do we use to do magick?

2. How long do Witches practice their magick?

3. Why do Witches work to keep the natural earth safe?

4. Name one reason that someone might keep it a secret that they are a Witch.

5. Name one thing that might be harder for a Witch to do if they were keeping it a secret that they were a Witch.

6. What is the Witch's Rede?

7. What does it mean?

8. What is the Rule of Three?

9. What does it mean?

10. Name a purpose for a household Altar.

11. What is Karma?

Chapter 10: The Tools of a Witch

Witches use different tools for all of the things they do. Some of these tools look like ordinary objects, but they become magickal when we use them for our Witchcraft. Witches are very good at taking things they already own and turning them into their magickal tools.

Before you make or use any tools, the first thing you must do is think about **safety**. Child Witches must ***always*** have a grown-up with them when they are using magick or working with fire or sharp objects. If you don't follow this instruction, you could be *breaking the Witch's Rede* by harming yourself!

Though there are many kinds of tools that magickal people use; for now we are going to learn about ten of them: The Athame, the Book of Shadows, a Broom, Candles, the Cauldron, Crystals, a Witch's Hat, the Pentagram, the Witch's Robe, and the magick Wand.

The **Athame** (ath-uh-may) is a knife that has a black handle and an edge on both sides. Witches use their athame during rituals to draw their magick circle in the air and to write words on candles.

The **Book of Shadows** is the Witch's magick book. This is where we write down our spells and our dreams and all of our magickal work.

Our **Broom** is also called a **Besom** (beh-sum). This is different than our household broom. A Witch's broom is used to clean away any bad energy from our ritual area before we perform our magick.

Candles come in different colors and shapes, and we use these differences in our magick spells. We almost always use candles when we do magick. Many times we write words or symbols and rub oils or herbs onto the candles we use.

Our **Cauldron** is a pot with three legs. The top of the pot is smaller and the bottom is round. Witches use their cauldrons to cook and make their potions in.

Crystals are stones that come in different colors. They come from the earth and they have a deep connection to both the energy of the Universe and the energy of people. Witches use them to connect to their own powers, and to bring healing, love, protection, and other magick to themselves.

The **Witch's Hat** has been around for over two thousand years. It is shaped like a cone because, like a pyramid, the top of the cone points up to the Heavens and the Deities. This helps to bring the powers of the Goddess and God down into the Witch and helps their magick grow stronger.

The **Pentagram** is a star inside of a circle. This is a very powerful symbol of a Witch, and it brings good luck and protection to the Witch who wears it. The five points of the star stand for: *fire, water, earth, air, and spirit.*

A **Witch's Robe** is a magickal covering. It can be any color, and can have designs or symbols. What is really special about wearing a Witch's Robe is that it helps you to concentrate on your magick and makes you focus on who you are.

The magick **Wand** is a favorite tool of many Witches. It is like a part of the Witch's body. When you point it, you are pointing your energy out or receiving the energy of the world into you. Wands are usually made of wood, but they can also be made of crystals or metals.

What have we learned? There are many tools that a Witch uses in their life and with their magick. We can make tools out of ordinary objects, and they will become magickal when we decide to use them in our magickal studies.

The first and most important part about working with magick is our safety. Children must always have an adult working with them.

The **Athame** is a knife that is used during ritual and magick.

The **Book of Shadows** is a magickal diary full of the secrets of the Witch who owns it.

Our **Broom** is used only for magick and not household cleaning. Another name for the broom is a **Besom**.

Candles are almost always used in magick and they come in many different colors.

Our **Cauldron** is a pot that we cook in during magick.

Crystals are magickal stones that bring Witches power.

A **Witch's Hat** is shaped like a cone because it focuses the power of the Goddess and God down into the Witch wearing it.

The **Pentagram** is a star that protects the Witch. It stands for fire, water, earth, air, and spirit.

A **Witch's Robe** helps the Witch focus on who they are and what they are doing when they perform magick.

The magick **Wand** is a part of the Witch's body and it directs energy in and out of the Witch during magick.

Questions

1. What is the first and most important part of working magick?

2. What must child Witches do before working magick?

3. What is a Witch's magickal diary called?

4. Do Witches use candles very often?

5. What is an Athame?

6. What is another name for the Witch's Broom?

7. What do crystals do for the Witch?

8. What do Witches cook in?

9. What is the shape of the Witch's Hat?

10. Why is the Witch's Hat so important?

11. Why do Witches wear Robes?

12. Which tool is like a part of the Witch's body?

13. What does the magick Wand do during magick?

14. What symbol brings good luck and protection to a Witch?

15. What do the five points of a Pentagram stand for?

Chapter 11: Rituals and Prayers

Witches spend a lot of time praying and performing rituals. We value our relationship with the God and Goddess as one of the most important things in our lives. Prayers and rituals help us to talk with them and grow closer to them.

When we pray, we are talking directly to the God and Goddess. We can say a prayer anytime and anywhere; all we have to do is concentrate on the Deities and start talking. You can talk out loud or to yourself; either way, the God and Goddess will hear you. Some of the reasons we pray are:

- To feel close to the God and Goddess.
- To ask the God and Goddess for help.
- To thank the God and Goddess for the things that you have.

We perform rituals to make sacred, special places in our home or work area so that we can perform magick. There are many ways to perform rituals, but the *reasons* for doing rituals are all about connecting with the Goddesses and Gods and the energy of the Universe.

Everything in the world is connected: all of the earth, air, water, fire and spirit in the Universe are connected; and when we do rituals we are using the power of all of those things. Our rituals are about our feelings, and working up those emotions towards what kind of magick we are performing. This is what gives our spells their energy. We picture what we want and concentrate as hard as we can until we **believe** that it has already come true. It's kind of like being really, really hyper – but on the inside.

The Steps for Performing a Ritual

First, we **"clean" our work area**. This is one of the times we Witches use our magick brooms. We sweep all of the bad energy out of the area.

Next, we **cast our circle**. Our circle is a magick place. Once we have made it, no bad energy can get in, and your powerful energy won't get out. We draw our circle in the air with our *athame*, or on the ground with salt or chalk or something like that. We stand in the center and draw our circle around us, turning clockwise.

After our circle is drawn, we **call the Quarters**. This means we are calling Guardians to come and watch over us during our ritual. There are many different kinds of Guardians and you can choose which ever you would like to work with. The Quarters are also sometimes called *Watchtowers*. Other Guardians include: Angels, Spirit Guides, Dragons, and many more. When we ask them to come, we face in different directions and call out to them. First we face the east, then south, west, and north. There are always four Guardians to call: one for each direction.

Next, we **invoke the Deity** we want to work with. You can call the Mother Goddess or Father God, or you can call one of the many Goddesses and Gods. This is when it is good to know what each of the Gods and Goddesses are strong at. *Always be polite to them*!

Now is when we **raise the energy** for our magick. That really hyper-on-the-inside feeling when we concentrate on what we want and we see it actually happening is a very important part of the ritual. Sometimes we raise energy by dancing; sometimes by chanting. You can raise energy any way that works for you.

What is **the purpose of your ritual**? It is time to tell the Universe and the Deities you are working with what you are working this ritual for. If you have a spell to do, this is when to do it. This is the "main event" of the whole ritual, so make it special!

When you are finished performing your ritual, you must **ground your energy**. This is sort of like *coming back to earth*. Imagine that all of the energy you built up inside you is now falling out of your feet and into the ground.

Then, remember to **thank the Deity** you are working with! After that you can **release the Guardians** and thank them too.

Finally, you must **release the circle**. Do you remember how you drew the circle by walking around it clockwise? To release the circle, point your athame outward and even with your circle, and walk around it counter-clockwise and say: *"This circle is open, but not broken"*.

Now you are free to walk outside of the circle. You should do something ordinary to help you feel close to the real world again. Many Witches do this by eating and drinking to celebrate the ritual they just performed.

What have we learned? Prayer and ritual are big parts of a Witch's life. We use prayer and ritual to talk to the Goddess and God and to grow closer to them.

Prayers are our way to talk directly to the Goddess and God at any time of the day. We can talk to them about anything, including: asking for help and thanking them for the good things in our life.

Rituals make our homes and work areas sacred and powerful for our magick. Rituals connect us to the Deities and to their energy. The whole Universe is connected, and we can use the power of everything to do magick. The steps in a ritual are:

- Cleaning our work area: we sweep away bad energy.
- Casting our circle: we trace or draw our circle in a clockwise direction.
- Calling the Quarters: these are four Guardians that stand at each of the directions – east, south, west and north.
- Invoking the Deity: we call which ever Deity we wish to ask for help or guidance.
- Raising energy: we concentrate on our goal so hard that we believe it's already happened. The energy feels like we are in a really hyper mood. We dance or chant or sing to raise energy.

- Stating the purpose of the ritual: now we do our spells.
- Grounding our energy: coming back down to earth.
- Thank the Deity: we are always grateful and polite.
- Release the Guardians: we say thank you and let them go.
- Release the circle: we trace our circle again, but in a counter-clockwise direction. Now we can leave the circle.

Questions

1. If we want to talk to the God and Goddess for a little while, what should we do?

2. What do rituals create in our homes?

3. Who do rituals connect us to?

4. Which parts of the Universe are connected?

5. How do we usually clean our work area before a ritual?

6. What direction do we trace our circle when we are creating it?

7. How many Guardians do we call for in a ritual?

8. Where do the Guardians stand?

9. Why do we invoke a Deity during a ritual?

10. What does raising energy feel like?

11. At what part of the ritual do we do our spells?

12. What do we do to come back down to earth?

13. Before we can leave the circle what do we have to do?

14. What direction do we walk in to release the circle?

Chapter 12: The Elements

All life is made up of five elements: earth, air, water, fire, and spirit. Everything you see, hear, touch, taste, and smell is an element. Each of the elements has its own "personality" and can be described by any of these. There is a color, a direction and a physical creature assigned to each element. There are even *people* that represent the elements. You can tell which element you are by your zodiac sign - or when you were born. We use the elements in our rituals and spells; their differences bring special qualities to our magick.

Earth

The color of the element earth is **green**.
The direction of the element earth is **north**.
The creature of the element earth is the **gnome**.
The zodiac signs of the element earth are **Taurus**, **Virgo** and **Capricorn**.

The element earth stands for: **growth, stability, abundance, prosperity**, and **beauty**.

Air

The color of the element air is **yellow**.
The direction of the element air is **east**.
The creature of the element air is the
sylph.
The zodiac signs of the element air are
Gemini, **Libra** and **Aquarius**.

The element air stands for:
communication, **ideas**, **intelligence**,
divination, and **education**.

Water

The color of the element water is **blue**.
The direction of the element water is **west**.
The creature of the element water is the
water nymph.
The zodiac signs of the element water are
Cancer, **Scorpio** and **Pisces**.

The element water stands for: **emotions**,
intuition, **adaptability**, **mystery**, and
psychic energy.

Fire

The color of the element fire is **red**.
The direction of the element fire is **south**.
The creature of the element fire is the **salamander**.
The zodiac signs of the element fire are **Aries**, **Leo** and **Sagittarius**.

The element fire stands for: **the physical, courage, change, passion,** and **love**.

Spirit

Spirit is different than all of the other elements. Actually, spirit is the same as all of the other elements, too. Spirit does not have its own color or direction or creature or people. It has all of them. The element of spirit has all people, all creatures, and all things. Spirit is everywhere! We might be on different "teams" like fire or water, but in the beginning and in the end, we are all spirit!

What have we learned? Everything in the world is made up of the elements. The elements are: earth, air, water, fire and spirit. Some words that describe the elements:

<u>Earth</u> – green, north, the gnomes, Taurus, Virgo, Capricorn, growth, prosperity.

<u>Air</u> – yellow, east, the sylphs, Gemini, Libra, Aquarius, communication, intelligence.

<u>Water</u> – blue, west, the water nymphs, Cancer, Scorpio, Pisces, emotions, intuition.

<u>Fire</u> – red, south, the salamanders, Aries, Leo, Sagittarius, courage, the physical.

<u>Spirit</u> – Everything!

Questions

1. What are the five elements?

2. What are the colors of the elements?
    Earth -   Water –
    Air -   Fire –

3. What are the directions of the elements?
    Earth -   Water –
    Air -   Fire –

4. Which element is about intelligence?

5. Which element is about abundance?

6. Which element is about courage?

7. Which element is about intuition?

8. Where is spirit?

9. What is your zodiac sign?

10. Which element are you?

Chapter 13: Symbols and Talismans

Witches have a lot of magick in their lives. You already know about our tools, but some of us work with magickal **symbols** and **talismans** as well. We Witches like mystery and secrets and hidden knowledge. We know that the more mysterious something is, the stronger our imagination becomes. We know that the more secret our magick is, the more power there is in our spells. We know that the hidden knowledge in the world is waiting for us to discover it, so that we can grow that much closer to the Goddess and God. Magickal symbols and talismans help us to build our world in mystery, secrecy, and the hidden knowledge of the Universe.

Symbols

A symbol is a picture or drawing or mark that means something special to the person who has it. There are different kinds of symbols and different reasons for using them.

When we draw a symbol onto something, we are making it powerful. Every time we see the symbol we think of our magick, and that makes the magick stronger.

Witches use symbols on their tools, objects, clothes, and diaries. Two examples of the symbols we use are: **sigils** and **magickal alphabets**.

Sigils are symbols that represent a person or thing. You can use a sigil that already exists, or you can make one up. For example, a round circle with short lines coming out of the sides means the sun; or you can make up a different picture to mean the sun that only you will know about. Get it? Once you decide what that symbol will mean for you, you can use it to focus on when you do magick. A lot of sigils use numbers in the pictures. These numbers are like phone numbers to the Deities who are going to work with you on your magick.

There are many **magickal alphabets** that Witches use. We use them to keep our magick secret and to make it powerful. Sometimes we use these alphabets to write in our *Book of Shadows* and to write our names and spells on our tools.

Talismans

A talisman is a drawing or object – like a statue or a necklace – that we carry for good luck or for part of our magickal work. Anything can be a talisman. Some examples of talismans are: a rabbit's foot, a lucky coin, a favorite outfit that you always wear on important occasions, or a stuffed animal that protects you from bad dreams while you sleep. The longer you own a talisman and the more you think about the power it brings to you, the more magickal it becomes. A talisman has power when you *believe* it does.

The Theban Alphabet
(A popular magickal alphabet)

Symbol	Letter	Symbol	Letter	Symbol	Letter
ᶈ	A	ᶙ	I	ᶕ	Q
ᶑ	B	ᶙ	J	ᶢ	R
ᶆ	C	ᶗ	K	ᶚ	S
ᶏ	D	ᶎ	L	ᶗ	T
ᶐ	E	ᶘ	M	ᶅ	U
ᶖ	F	ᶓ	N	ᶅ	V
ᶙ	G	ᶗ	O	ᶍ	W
ᶖ	H	ᶛ	P	ᶙ	X
				ᶘ	Y
				ᶗ	Z

What have we learned? Magickal symbols and talismans are some more examples of the tools that Witches use. Three of the reasons we use symbols and talismans are because of the mystery and secrecy and hidden knowledge they bring to our lives. Our imaginations grow stronger when we use these mysterious, magickal tools.

A symbol is a picture that means something else. Symbols make things powerful and help us to concentrate. Two types of symbols we use are sigils and magickal alphabets. Sigils sometimes have numbers in them and magickal alphabets are used to write in secret languages. A popular magickal alphabet is the Theban Alphabet.

A talisman is like a lucky charm: we can make any object that we own our personal talisman. Talismans work because we believe they do.

Questions

1. When something is mysterious, it helps our imagination to do what?

2. Name one of the reasons we use symbols and talismans.

3. What is a symbol?

4. Name two different kinds of symbols.

5. Sigils that use numbers are like phone numbers to whom?

6. Sometimes we use a magickal alphabet to write in our

   _____.

7. Write your name in the Theban Alphabet.

   _____.

8. Why does a talisman have power?

Chapter 14: Herbology

Herbology is the study of herbs and plants. Herbs are any plant or tree, and all of their parts, which can be used for food or medicine. When we use herbs for food and medicine we are using the energy that is inside the plant and making it work with our own energy and power.

Herbs are strongest when they are grown naturally and are fresh. Many Witches keep their own herb gardens – both inside and outdoors. Many of us believe that we bring more power to our herbs if we harvest (or pick) them on certain days and at certain times, or if we have raised our magickal energy first. We always handle herbs with care and respect.

How do herbs work? Herbs help our bodies clean themselves on the inside. They work with our bodies naturally so that we can begin to heal ourselves and so that our energy will grow stronger. Not all herbs work right away, but they work over time to put our bodies back in touch with nature. Have you ever heard anyone say "An apple a day keeps the doctor away"? Well, that is how a lot of herbs work. A little bit a day, makes your body okay! Herbs have a lot of vitamins and they wake up our insides so that our magickal energy will be at its best.

There are many ways to use herbs. Once an herb is harvested it can be prepared in any number of ways, depending upon what you wish to use the herb for. Each of these ways is good for different purposes. Here are a few examples:

- **Infusions** - A beverage. Usually a tea. This can be hot or cold. The herb is boiled in water to make the infusion.

- **Powders** - Dried plants. Once the herb is dried out, it is ground into a fine power and is usually added to food.

- **Ointments** - Like lotions. The herbs are added to oil or creams and then used on the skin.

- **Herb Baths** - First fill a cloth bag with the herb you will be using and boil in water to release the power of the herb. Then add the bag of herbs and the boiled water to your regular bath water just before you get in.

- **Incense** - Herbs that are burned for their scent. These bring special energies into a room.

- **Poppets and Sachets** – Poppets are dolls and Sachets are bags. They are both sewn out of cloth and filled with herbs. They are used to work magick and are carried as talismans.

Safety

One more time: What is the most important thing to remember when you are working with magick? *Safety comes first!* Even when you are using herbs for medicine instead of magick, you must **always** have an adult help you.

Some important safety rules you **must** remember before you begin to study Herbology:

1. Medicine is something that doctors and grownups give you; not something you give yourself.

2. Just because something is natural, doesn't make it safe. There are a lot of poisonous plants in the world. Even grownups shouldn't work with plants until they know everything about the ones they want to work with.

3. Children must never use fire, boiling water, or herbs without their parent's help. No one, not even grown-ups, should drink or eat or rub onto their skin

<u>anything</u> that they don't know <u>everything</u> about.

4. Study, study, study! There is a lot to learn in the world of Herbology. A wise Witch studies with books first before they ever start to use real herbs.

A Few Common and Useful Herbs

Catnip

* Catnip comes from the mint family.
* Catnip makes cats excited, but it scares
  away bugs.

Magickal Uses: Use catnip in spells for love,
beauty and happiness. Drinking catnip tea
can help you with your tarot card studies.
Burning catnip incense will help you with
bad habits.

Medical Uses: Catnip is used for relaxation,
for fighting the stomach flu, and to help get
rid of colds. Chewing on catnip leaves will
help a toothache.

Chamomile

* Chamomile is one of the most popular
  herbs in herb gardens.
* Chamomile flowers smell like apples.

Magickal Uses: Chamomile is useful in
spells for money, sleep and protection.
Chamomile is strongly connected to all Sun
Gods and will help when you are calling
upon them for your magick.

Medical Uses: Chamomile will help a person to relax, and is often drunk as a tea. You can also use Chamomile while making bath oils or skin lotions for relaxation spells. Chamomile can also calm down an angry person.

Ginger Root

* Ginger is used quite a lot in the kitchen.
* There are many different types of ginger, and only some can be used in magick and medicine.

Magickal Uses: Ginger is useful in spells for protection and for healing magick. Ginger Roots often grow into shapes that look like people. These make very powerful talismans.

Medical Uses: Ginger tea can help you get over an upset stomach. Ginger is also used for muscle pains and sprains. Ginger will help you feel better when you have a sore throat or cough.

Kava Kava

* Kava Kava has been made as a popular drink for thousands of years.
* Kava Kava comes from the black pepper family.

Magickal Uses: Kava Kava will help you to remember your dreams. Some cultures believe that Kava Kava can help you communicate with the Gods.

Medical Uses: Kava Kava relaxes your muscles. It is used often to help people sleep or to make them less nervous. Kava Kava is another herb that is good to ease pain.

Passion Flower

* The fruit of the Passion Flower looks like a yellow egg and can be eaten.
* This fruit is a popular food in the tropical rainforest.

Magickal Uses: Burning Passion Flower incense will change the energy in the room and will get rid of any anger or stress that is around. Passion Flower will help with spells for peace and friendship and will bring calm to people who use it.

Medical Uses: Passion Flower is another herb that relaxes muscles that are tense and eases nerve pains. It works well for some infections and viruses. Passion Flower is also used in some creams and make-up that help keep the skin young.

Sage

* The name Sage comes from the Latin word salvia, which means "healthy".

Magickal Uses: Some say that Sage is an herb of immortality and will keep a person young and healthy forever. Sage does keep the mind and memory strong and wise. Sage can also be used to banish evil and to bring well-being and wishes into our lives.

Medical Uses: Sage can be used as a tea for stomach pains. You can use Sage in lotions to rub into wounds. If you have a sore throat, it will help to gargle with Sage.

What have we learned? Herbology is the study of herbs and plants. We use herbs in food and medicine. When we use herbs for magick we are using their energy along with our own. Herbs are more powerful when they are fresh and so, many Witches like to grow and harvest their own herb gardens.

There are many ways to use herbs. An infusion is something we drink after boiling herbs in water. When we dry herbs and crush them we are making a powder. When we add herbs to creams or oil, we are making an ointment which can be used as a lotion. When you use herbs to make an herbal bath you should put the herbs in a cloth bag and boil them in water to activate the energy of the herbs; and then add the bag and the water to your bath. Herbs that are burned for their smell are being used as incense. When you sew cloth up into the shape of a doll or a small bag and fill it with herbs, you are making a poppet or sachet. These can be used in magick spells or as talismans.

Herbs work by healing our bodies naturally and helping our magickal energy grow stronger.

Safety is the first rule when studying herbs. We should always read as much as we can about an herb before we actually work with it; and children should never use herbs without a grown-up's help.

Questions

1. What is Herbology the study of?

2. We use herbs in food and
   _____.

3. What does it mean to "harvest" herbs?

4. What is an **infusion** of herbs?

5. What two things do you have to do to an herb to make a powder?

6. Which type of herbal mixture do you rub on your skin?

7. When you use herbs as incense what are you burning them for?

8. A cloth doll that is filled with herbs is called a _____.

9. A cloth bag that is filled with herbs is called a _____.

10. Name one of the ways that herbs work.

11. What is the most important rule when working with Herbology?

12. What does a wise Witch do first – before actually working with herbs?

Chapter 15: Animal Magick

Most cultures believe that there is a connection between people and animals. Witches know that this is true. We know that everything in the world is connected, and that includes all animals. Many people believe that animals are even more spiritual and powerful than humans, and that they are closer to the Mother Earth and to the God and Goddess. This is why Witches work with animals: *because they can bring power to our lives and teach us a lot about our magick.*

A Witch's **Familiar** is a pet that has a special connection with them. Most people think of cats when they hear the word, but a Witch's Familiar can be *any* animal. Witches believe that because their Familiars are so close to nature, they make our magick and our rituals special.

Magickal people also work with **Power Animals**. These are animals or animal spirits that have specific qualities and strengths. While Familiars are individual animals, Power Animals are symbols of the whole species. So if your familiar is a bird, then that bird is probably a pet that lives with you. If your Power Animal is a bear, then all bears are your Power Animal and the spirit of one of them is always with you; just like a spirit guide.

We all have a Power Animal, and when we use our imaginations to see and communicate with ours, we can learn from them. Different animals have their own special qualities, and when we need one of those to help us we can call on the power of our animal. We can connect with the animal energy that is inside of us and take on some of their power as our own. Our Power Animal is our guardian and is there to protect us. Sometimes an entire family or group will also have a Power Animal that watches over and guards them all.

Do you know what your Power Animal is? There are several ways you can discover yours. Do you ever dream of a particular animal? Maybe you have a special favorite? You should pay very close attention to these and look up the magickal meanings of those animals. Once you've discovered your Power Animal you will make yourself a powerful protection talisman if you keep a likeness of it; like a carving or a picture or a stuffed animal.

No matter what kind of animals enter our lives or which animals we work with, Witches respect them all; just as we respect other people, and nature, and everything else that the Goddess and God have created.

What have we learned? There is a connection between people and animals. Witches work with animals because they can bring power to our lives and teach us a lot about our magick. Some people consider animals to be even more spiritual and powerful than humans.

A **Familiar** is a pet that has a special connection with the Witch it belongs to. The Familiar is a specific, individual animal.

Our **Power Animal** is an animal or animal spirit that has a special connection with us and protects us. The Power Animal represents the entire species of that animal. Everyone has a Power Animal. We can call upon the power of ours if we need their strength. If we connect with the animal energy that is inside of us we will take on some of the power of our Power Animal.

Some people dream about their Power Animal and some of us just have a special favorite that we already feel close to.

Keeping an object with our Power Animal on it, like a stuffed animal or a statue or a picture will give us protection.

Questions

1. Why do Witches work with animals?

2. What do you call a Witch's pet that has a special connection to them?

3. Why do Witches believe that Familiars make their magick and rituals special?

4. A _____ is an animal or animal spirit that has specific qualities and _____.

5. A Power Animal is not an individual animal, but a symbol of what?

6. If we want to take on some of the power of our Power Animal, what do we need to connect with?

7. What is your Power Animal?

Chapter 16: Divination

Divination is the art of foretelling the future. People have been using signs and tools and psychic intuition to predict what will happen to them since the beginning of the human race. **Intuition** is when you *"just know"* something. When we practice divination we are discovering knowledge that we already have inside of us. All of us are a part of everything else in the universe. We are connected to it all. When we use our psychic abilities to practice divination we are seeing patterns in the way things are connected and the way that life is moving around us.

When we use fortune-telling tools to practice divination we are connecting with the Deity inside of us and with our spirit guides. There are many different kinds of tools that we can use, and they work by giving us something to focus on so that our intuition can guide us. The more we practice divination the stronger our intuition will grow.

A Few of the Tools We Use for Divination

Astrology

Astrology is the study of where the planets are in the sky and how they are moving around the Earth; and of the effects this has on the world and on people. The areas that the planets were in at the exact moment you were born will tell you a lot about your personality. Once you begin to study more about astrology you will be able to use the movements of the planets to predict future events in your life.

The first part of your own astrology chart that you will learn about is your **Sun Sign**. This is where the sun was during the month that you were born. This is the sign that you read when you are looking at your horoscope. Look below to find your Sun Sign and circle it.

Sun Sign (Birthdays)Personality Traits

Aries (March 21-April 19)	Original, Courageous, Direct
Taurus (April 20-May 20)	Patient, Reliable, Affectionate
Gemini (May 21-June 21)	Intellectual, Lively, Funny
Cancer (June 22-July 22)	Kind, Sensitive, Imaginative
Leo (July 23-August 22)	Generous, Creative, Enthusiastic
Virgo (August 23-September 22)	Practical, Modest, Clean
Libra (September 23-October 22)	Charming, Social, Artistic
Scorpio (October 23 - November 21)	Loyal, Determined, Passionate
Sagittarius (November 22-December 21)	Optimistic, Moral, Funny
Capricorn (December 22-January 19)	Cautious, Ambitious, Patient
Aquarius (January 20-February 18)	Activist, Friendly, Modern
Pisces (February 19-March 20)	Mystical, Intuitive, Sympathetic

Numerology

Numerology is the study of numbers. There are many ways to use numerology. The two most common ways are in reading your **Birth Number** - *which reveals your talents and life path*; and your **Name Number** - *which reveals your personality*.

To find these you have to do a little math. You assign a number to each letter in your name or birthday and then add up all of the numbers. Once you have one large number, you add those new numbers. You keep doing this until you have a single number between 1 and 9, or until you have the number 11 or 22. When you are ready you will use the key below. First look at the example below the key to see how it is done. (There are brief meanings for your Name Numbers on the next page to show you how this works.)

1	2	3	4	5	6	7	8	9
A	B	C	D	E	F	G	H	I
J	K	L	M	N	O	P	Q	R
S	T	U	V	W	X	Y	Z	

Example:
Name:

L o r i n D a r l e e n M a n d e r l y
3+6+9+9+5 + 4+1+9+3+5+5+5 + 4+1+5+4+5+9+3+7 = 102

$102 = \underline{1+0+2} = \boxed{3}$

Birthday:

03/18/1970 (March 18, 1970)

$3+ 1+8 + 1+9+7+0 = 29 = 2+9 = \boxed{11}$

Interpretations for Name Numbers

1 = independent, and can take care of themselves.

2 = clever, and investigative.

3 = cheerful, and light-hearted.

4 = conventional, and down-to-earth.

5 = brave, and exciting.

6 = take-charge, and home-loving.

7 = spiritual, and eccentric.

8 = take-charge, and success-driven.

9 = good at many things, and has many interests.

11 = educated, and excitable.

22 = ambitious, and a world leader.

Tarot Cards

Tarot cards are a fun and popular way to work with Divination. There are hundreds of different styles of cards, but they are all cards with pictures on them. These pictures are signs about the events that happen in life and on our path of growing up. Our moods, our successes, and our problems are all inside of a Tarot deck.

Each deck has **78** cards in it. There are **22 Major Arcana** that are numbered **0-21**, and there are **56 Minor Arcana** that are divided into four groups like a regular deck of playing cards. Instead of hearts, diamonds, clubs, and spades though, a Tarot deck has **cups**, **pentacles (or coins)**, **wands**, and **swords**. Each group has ten cards numbered **Ace** through **Ten** and four cards that are the **Page**, **Knight**, **Queen**, and **King**.

All of the cards in the Major Arcana have their own meaning. Each of the cards in the Minor Arcana has a double meaning, and is influenced by the numbers and the suits.

Major Arcana

0 – The Fool: Innocence

1 – The Magician: Creativity

2 – The High Priestess: Wisdom

3 – The Empress: Mother figure

4 – The Emperor: Father figure

5 – The Hierophant: Tradition

6 – The Lovers: Love

7 – The Chariot: Work and travel

8 – Strength: Power

9 – The Hermit: Meditation

10 – Wheel of Fortune: Fortune

11 – Justice: Fairness

12 – The Hanged Man: Suspense

13 – Death: Sudden change

14 – Temperance: Patience

15 – The Devil: Bad behavior

16 – The Tower: Rethinking your beliefs

17 – The Star: Hope

18 – The Moon: Mystery

19 – The Sun: Success

20 – Judgment: Reward

21 – The World: Triumph

Minor Arcana

Cups: Emotions **Pentacles**: Money **Wands**: Work
Swords: Problems

King - An older man

Queen - An older woman

Knight - A young man or woman

Page - A younger boy or girl

Ten – Hesitation

Nine – Contentment

Eight – Organization

Seven – Imagination

Six - Victory

Five - Challenge

Four - Energy

Three - Appreciation

Two - Commitment

Ace - New beginnings

To use the Tarot cards for Divination you shuffle the deck while thinking of a question that you would like answers for. Then you take the cards from the deck that you are going to use and place them before you in what is called a Tarot **Spread**.

You put a certain number of cards down in a spread, and then you read the meanings of each of the cards in the spread. When the meanings of all the cards in your spread are put together they will give you your answer. Sometimes you will have to think a while in order to understand the answer you receive.

Pendulums

Pendulums are used to answer yes-or-no questions. They can be made with a crystal, stone, or metal object and some string. The object of choice is attached to a string that is long enough to let the crystal, stone, or metal swing freely. The ends of the string are held away from the diviner's body so that the object can hang down.

Once you have a Pendulum that you would like to use, hold it out away from your body with your fingertips by the ends of the string. Do your best to stop any movement. Now you are going to ask out loud: "What is the answer for 'yes'?" The Pendulum will eventually start to move again. Let the Pendulum move how it wants to, and don't try to control the direction it moves in. You do want to pay attention to how it is moving though. It will usually move either from right to left or forward and back again. Then, ask aloud: "What is the answer for 'no'?" You will usually get the opposite movement of the answer you got for "yes".

Pendulums are fun and easy to use. They are also easy to make! You can even use a ring from your finger and a piece of thread!

Runes

Runes are symbols. They can be carved on talismans, candles, and other objects, or written on paper for the power that each symbol brings, or they can be used as a language. Each Rune has its own letter and its own magickal meaning.

When used in Divination, each symbol is carved or drawn on a stone or other object and then placed in a bag. You then concentrate on the question you have and mix up the bag of Runes. Like you did with the Tarot cards, you are going to pick a certain numbers of Runes and place them on the table in front of you. There are several meanings for each Rune for you to learn as you study them more. For now, here is a chart of the most common type of Rune language used, along with their name, their pronunciation and the letter they stand for.

Rune	Name and Pronunciation	Letter
ᚠ	Fehu "fay-who"	F
ᚢ	Uruz "ooo-rooze"	U
ᚦ	Thurisaz "thoor-ee-saws"	TH

ᚠ	Ansuz "awn-sooze"	A
ᚱ	Raidho "rye- though"	R
ᚲ	Kenaz "kane-awze"	K OR C
ᚷ	Gebo "gay-boe"	G
ᚹ	Wunjo "woon-yo"	W OR V
ᚺ	Hagalaz "haw-gaw-laws"	H
ᚾ	Nauthiz "now-these"	N
ᛁ	Isa "ee-saw"	I
ᛃ	Jera "yare-awe"	J or Y

ᛇ   Eihwaz "eye-wawz"   EI

ᛈ   Perthro "perth-row"   P

ᛉ   Algiz "all-yeese"   Z or R

ᛊ   Sowilo "soe-wee-low"   S

ᛏ   Tiwaz „tea-wawz"   T

ᛒ   Berkano „bear-kawn-oh"   B

ᛖ   Ehwaz „ay-wawz"   E

ᛗ   Mannaz „mawn-nawz"   M

ᛚ   Laguz „law-gooze"   L

◇ Ingwaz „eeeng-wawz" NG

ᛗ Dagaz "thaw-gauze" D

ᛟ Othala "oath-awe-law" O

Crystal Balls

This is called **Scrying**. Pictures seem to appear when you stare into a crystal and let your mind relax. You interpret these pictures. When you practice this kind of divination you should be somewhere very quiet, as it takes a lot of concentration. Keep your mind blank. Try to think of nothing at all. After a lot of practice you will begin to see pictures that you will need to interpret. Write down what you see or whatever comes to your mind. When you are done Scrying, you can go back to what you've written and work on what each picture means.

There are many different ways to practice Divination. Most Witches practice some form or another. It's good to know at least a little about all of them. You should also pick your favorites to study more about and that you can use in your daily magickal practices.

What have we learned? Divination is the art of foretelling the future. **Intuition** is when you "just know" something. The knowledge that we get when we use Divination is already inside of us. The more we practice Divination, the stronger our intuition grows.

Astrology is the study of the planets and how they move. The areas where the planets are when we are born tell a lot about our personality. Our **Sun Sign** is what we read when we look up our horoscope. Our Sun Sign is where the Sun was the month we were born.

Numerology is the study of numbers. Two common numerology readings are the **Birth Number** and the **Name Number** readings. Our Birth Number describes our talents and life path, and our Name Number describes our personality. To find any numerology number we have to do math. We have to add up the numbers that are assigned to the letters in our name or the numbers in our birthday, and keep adding these numbers together until we have a single digit **1-9** or the number **11** or **22**.

Tarot Cards are cards with pictures on them that relate to the things going on in our lives. There are **78** cards in a Tarot deck: **22 Major Arcana** and **56 Minor Arcana**. The Major Arcana each have their own meaning and are numbered 0-21. There are four suits in the Minor Arcana: **cups, pentacles, wands,** and **swords**. The Minor Arcana cards are numbered **Ace-10,** and **Page, Knight, Queen,** and **King**. The meanings of the Minor Arcana are influenced by the numbers and the suits. When you shuffle the deck and place some of the cards in front of you, you are making a **Tarot Card Spread**.

Pendulums are used to answer yes-or-no questions and are made with string and a crystal, stone, or metal object.

Runes are symbols that have magickal meanings. They also stand for letters of the alphabet and are an ancient language.

When you gaze into a **crystal ball** you are **scrying**. To scry, you must concentrate quietly and wait to see what pictures come to the crystal or to your mind. Then you must work out the meanings of the pictures you have seen.

Questions

1. What is Divination?

2. What is Intuition?

3. What is Astrology the study of?

4. What do we read for our horoscope?

5. What is your own Sun Sign?

6. What is a personality trait of your Sun Sign?

7. What is Numerology?

8. What are the two most common numerology readings?

9. What does the Birth Number reading tell?

10. What does the Name Number reading tell?

11. What is your Birth Number? What is your Name Number?

12. How many cards are in a Tarot Deck?

13. What are the four suits of the Minor Arcana?

14. What is a Tarot Card Spread?

15. What kind of questions do we use pendulums for?

16. What tool of divination is also an ancient language?

17. What is Scrying?

Chapter 17: Potions

A **Potion** is a liquid mixture of herbs and other ingredients that have been soaked in water for magickal or medicinal use. **Potioncraft** is what we are doing when we make and use potions for magickal or medicinal reasons.

We sometimes use the word **Brew** for our mixtures. The only difference between these is that the word **Brew** is used for magickal drinks, and **Potion** is used for medicinal concoctions. Another name you might hear for potions is: Wort.

Some potions are made by taking dried herbs and grounding them into a very fine power. These are called **Powder Potions** and are usually for sprinkling on objects – not for drinking. We also ground up herbs into powders or small pieces so that we can add them into our potion in a cauldron or pot. After adding the herbs we simmer the brew and then strain the pieces of herbs out when it is finished. For cold potions you would soak the herbs in cold water for several hours.

There are some kinds of potions that are <u>not</u> meant for drinking. We make some potions for our baths, for lotions, and for our household.

It's very important to know how each ingredient in your potion works and what kind of magick each has, so you will know how each of them will affect the potion. Never use poisonous ingredients or anything that will hurt yourself or others in your potions!

There are two things you must do before you actually begin to make potions. First, you must study the art of Potioncraft and learn all of the steps that are involved in making potions. Then, you must study all of the ingredients that you will be using. You need to know what each one of them does and how they will work together before you start actually working with them. Finally, you can begin to work with potions. Don't be in a hurry to get to this final step! It is much better for your magick if you are very well educated before beginning to practice!

Making a potion is like cooking. You will be following a recipe. It is important to follow that recipe very carefully. You have to get everything exactly right or the potion will not work the way you want it to. After you are more advanced in your studying you will learn to create your own potions, but for now, always follow your recipes carefully.

The tools you will need to make your potions are:

A bowl – to mix our herbs and other ingredients in.
A pot – to do our cooking in.
A wooden spoon – to stir our potions with.
A cloth strainer – so that we can strain out the pieces of herbs when our potion is finished simmering.
A mortar and pestle – this is what we use to grind up our herbs.
Containers – to put our potions into.
Ingredients – which we can grow or buy. Sometimes we use fresh herbs and sometimes we need them dried. Each ingredient brings its own magickal quality to the potion.
Water – is better when it is spring water or filtered.

In order for our potions to work magickally we have to make them at the right time. This means on the right day, at the right time of day, and during the right phase of the moon.

Once you have all of your ingredients together in your pot, you will simmer, stir, or steep – as your recipe tells you to. When you stir, always stir clockwise. This is the same as when we were creating a ritual circle. Remember? Clockwise was creating. You will lose the energy of your potion if you stir counter-clockwise.

When you are stirring you should concentrate on sending your energy into your potion. The simmering will release the magickal properties, and you will put that magick power to use with the three necessary steps a Witch must add to Potioncraft:

Intention: There needs to be a reason for this potion to exist, and you must have exactly what you are trying to do in your mind.
Desire: You must *really* want this to work. You must *know* that it will. *Try to use your entire brain while you're concentrating on this!*
Empowerment: You have to put as much of your own personal power into this potion as you can. This means that you should be concentrating on your potion and what you want from it the entire time you are putting the ingredients together, stirring them together, and going through the steps of your ritual. Imagine the power of the God and

Goddess traveling through your body and out of your hands into the potion.

As you study Potioncraft you will find many old books and recipes. Some of these will be easier and more useful than others and some will require you to put in extra work, like saying blessings and reading rhymes. Whichever recipes you decide to use, Potioncraft, if it interests you, will be exciting and fun. Just remember: safety first, study second, and then you may carry on. No fire, no herbs, and no drinking magick potions for child Witches without adult supervision!

What have we learned? A **Potion** is a liquid mixture of herbs and other ingredients. **Potioncraft** is what we are doing when we make potions. Potions are also called **Brews** and **Worts**. Potions are used for magickal and medicinal reasons.

Power potions are sprinkled on objects and are not usually for drinking. We have to know what each ingredient is and how it works so that we will know which potions are safe. We should never use poisonous ingredients! To make decoctions and infusions we simmer herbs in a brew and then strain the herb pieces out.

Two things that we should do before we ever start to make potions are: learn all of the steps to make a potion, and study all of the ingredients we will be using. Making potions is like cooking. We are following a recipe with ingredients and instructions that must be followed carefully. It's important that we make our potions at the right time and on the right day. Potions should always be stirred clockwise.

The three necessary steps in Potioncraft are: intention, desire, and empowerment. Our intention is our reason for our potion; our desire is how much we want and believe our potion will work; and when we empower our potion we are putting our energy into it.

Safety is the most important step in Potioncraft!

Questions

1. What is a Potion?

2. What is Potioncraft?

3. What are two other names for Potions?

4. What two things should we do before we start to make any Potions?

5. Making a Potion is like _____ and we follow a _____.

6. What direction should Potions be stirred?

7. What are the three necessary steps in Potioncraft?

8. What do we mean by "our intention"?

9. What do we mean by "our desire"?

10. What do we mean by "our empowerment"?

Chapter 18: Spells

A **Spell** is a Witch's way of making something happen. When we are working a spell we are building up the power inside of us and focusing it into our wish so that the patterns in the world around us change. Just like when we make potions, spells are done by following a list of instructions. There are a few more steps to do, like rituals and meditation and saying rhymes; but we are still collecting ingredients, getting the timing right, and using the energy inside of us to make things happen.

When we perform a spell we are working with Deities. We are asking them for their help in getting something that we want. It's important that we know exactly what it is that we want before we start the spell and that we can say it clearly with words or see it clearly in our minds with pictures. When we do a spell we cannot be focused on too many things or be unsure of what we want. *We have to know exactly what we are asking for; we have to believe that the spell will get it for us; and we have to believe that we can make the spell happen.*

It is very important to remember that we only do good magick! Do you remember the Witch's Rede: "And it harms none, do what you will"? This is what that means. We can use magick to get what we want, but not if it hurts anyone or anything; even ourselves.

We also do not do magick of any kind for other people without their permission. It is not up to us to decide what is best for other people. Everyone gets to make their own decisions! Never make other people do or feel something that you want. This is against everything that Witches believe in.

The steps you should follow when working with spells are pretty much the same, no matter what kind of spell you are doing. The items you use and the words you read might be different, but you should use these steps most of the time:

1) **Get yourself and your altar space ready.** A lot of Witches like to take a bath first so that the daily dirt isn't getting in their way. You can also take some deep breaths or put on a favorite outfit or your Witch's cloak. Your altar space should be set up with the objects and ingredients that you plan to use so that you won't have to leave your spell to go and get anything. It's good to have an object that represents each of the elements on your altar. For example: a candle for fire, a cup of water, incense for air, and a pentacle for earth.

2) **Make a ritual circle around your work space and call upon the Goddess or God that you want to work with.** The circle around you and your altar will protect you during your spell or ritual.

3) **Work that magick!** This is when you light candles and incense and mix those ingredients and oils. Whatever type of magick spell you are working with will have the instructions for what to do. Sometimes the steps will be pretty simple and other times you will have more difficult spells to work. One of the easiest and most popular kinds of magick is Candle Magick. This lets you pick a specific color candle according to what type of spell you want to do. For example, for love you will burn pink candles and for money you will burn green candles. Candles help us to concentrate on what we want.

4) **Rhymes/Chants/Prayers.** If there is something to say, now is the perfect time to say it! When we use rhymes to say our magick spells it is because this is a great way to build up energy and focus it on what our spell is for. Energy is what makes this work, so put some power into those words!

* *Remember: Know your spell. Study your spell. Know what you need. Know your results.*

Once you are working your spell, you should follow the instructions exactly. After you have studied a lot more you will be able to rewrite spells or write your own, but for now you should be very careful to follow the spell that you've chosen as it is written.

Sometimes we have to wait for the spell to work. Most of the time magick does not work right away. We have to send our energy out into the world with our spell and then sit back and wait for it to come back to us. Also, there are times when magick works differently then we think it will.

You should keep a journal of the magick that you work. This can be in your Book of Shadows, or it can be a separate diary. Keep track of the spell that you worked and everything that you did. Write down the time, the day, and all of the objects and ingredients you used. Also write down what you want to happen, and how you felt during and after the spell. Later write down what happened because of your spell. Did it work the way you thought and hoped? Did it work a different way? Did it not work at all? If things turn out different than you had hoped, don't give up! It takes a lot of practice before we can work magick exactly the way we want to. This will all help you to keep track of what works for you and what doesn't. It will also be a good tool to use once you begin to write your own spells!

What have we learned? A spell is a Witch's way of making something happen. Working a spell is like making a potion: we are following a list of instructions. It's important that we know exactly what it is that we want before we start the spell. When we do a spell we cannot be focused on too many things or unsure of what we want. We have to know exactly what we are asking for; we have to believe that the spell will get it for us; and we have to believe that we can make the spell happen.

The Witch's Rede says "And it harms none, do what you will". This means we can use magick to get what we want, but not if it hurts anyone or anything. We do not do magick of any kind for other people without their permission.

There are basic steps that we follow to perform a spell:

1) **Get yourself and your altar space ready.**

2) **Make a ritual circle around your work space and call upon the Goddess or God that you want to work with.**

3) **Work that magick!**

4) **Rhymes/Chants/Prayers.**

Once we are working our spell, we should follow the instructions exactly. Sometimes we have to wait for the spell to work, and sometimes we might be surprised at how our spell works.

We should keep a record of our magick spells in a journal and keep track of everything we did. This will help us to learn what works for us and what doesn't.

Questions

1. What is a Spell?

2. Finish this sentence: "And it harms none,

_____

_____

3. Do spells always work right away?

4. What are some of the things you have to **know** before doing a spell?

5. Why do we say rhymes or chants sometimes during a spell?

6. What color candle would you burn during a love spell?

7. Name something that you might put on your altar to represent each element.

About the Author

Lorin Manderly is a thirty-something, nature-loving, Goddess-worshiping, conservative-radical, Eclectic-Witch who has been practicing since childhood. Though this is her first work to be published, she has been a writer all of her life and plans for this textbook to be the first in a series of books for child Witches. She is currently selling off her worldly possessions so she can backpack around Europe for a year while continuing her writing and planning a private school for children being raised Pagan.

Made in the USA
Lexington, KY
07 August 2014